VOYA Occasional Papers Series

Dorothy Broderick

The intent of

to cover topic

adolescents o

or studies that

zine articles ar... ... short for publication as mono-
graphs will be considered for publication in this
series. The editor invites your submissions.

1. *The Young Adult Librarian's Knowledge of and Attitudes About Sex* by Susan Steinfirst, 1989.
2. *Two Pioneers of Young Adult Library Services* by Patty Campbell, 1998.

Two Pioneers of Young Adult Library Services

Patty Campbell

VOYA Occasional Papers Series

The Scarecrow Press, Inc.
Lanham, Maryland, & London
1998

SCARECROW PRESS, INC.

Published in the United States of America
by Scarecrow Press, Inc.
4720 Boston Way
Lanham, Maryland 20706

4 Pleydell Gardens, Folkestone
Kent CT20 2DN, England

British Library Cataloguing in Publication Information Available

Library of Congress Cataloging-in-Publication Data

Campbell, Patricia J.
    Two pioneers of young adult library services / Patty Campbell.
      p.   cm. — (VOYA occasional paper series ; 2)
    Includes bibliographical references and index.
    ISBN 0-8108-3423-5 (alk. paper)
    1. Young adults' libraries—United States—History—20th century.
2. Williams, Mabel, 1887–   —Interviews. 3. Young adult services
librarians—New York (State)—New York—Interviews. 4. Edwards,
Margaret A. Fair Garden and the swarm of beasts. 5. Teenagers—
United States—Books and reading. 6. Public libraries—Services to
teenagers—New York (State)—New York—History—20th century.
7. New York Public Library—History—20th century.
    I. Title. II. Series.
    Z718.5.C36   1998
    027.62'6—dc21   98-34918
                                             CIP

Contents

Introduction

This is really an "Afterword," so I suggest you first read Campbell's insightful analysis of the beginnings of work with young adults in two major libraries. We need all the history we can acquire in these days of living in the here and now. Then return to this introduction to obtain a very personal view of how a beginning librarian was impacted in the early days of her career.

Life at the New York Public Library

In the fall of 1954 a good friend helped me pack my meager belongings in her car and drove me from my small Connecticut town to New York City. It was pouring and the wind was atrocious and only by reading the newspaper the next day did I learn that we had navigated our way through a hurricane. It was a fitting beginning for a young woman from a small New England town, who was about to embark on working at the New York Public Library in the Young Adult department while attending Columbia University in pursuit of a master's degree in library service.

Although I did not know it at the time, 1954 was the twenty-fifth consecutive year that the New York Public Library would publish *Books for the Teen Age*, one of the most prestigious selection tools in the Young Adult Library Services area. Thirteen years earlier, on April 30, 1941, NYPL had opened the Nathan Straus Library on 32nd Street as a branch exclusively for young people under the age of twenty-one. Eventually, the Young Adult department would move to the Donnell Library on 53rd Street when it opened in December 1955.

An old, yellowing working document Mabel Williams gave Mary K. Chelton during her interview sums up the firm philosophy the staff at NYPL had developed for this service. It reads, in part:

> Our whole philosophy has been built upon the conviction that one cannot categorize the young person as a student or reference user or reader of sea stories. Rather you meet him as an individual and give him all the kinds of aid he needs as stu-

dent, reference user, and reader of sea stories—the guidance of the "whole" boy or girl in all his or her needs and interests.

I missed Mabel Williams by a couple of years but her legacy was in good hands with Margaret Scoggin firmly in place, surrounded by Lillian Morrison, Elaine Simpson, and Esther Walls. Only someone who was there can appreciate the joy it was to be mentored by such a marvelous staff. I was privileged to attend a public lecture by Amelia Munson and the ending of the story she told that evening in the auditorium of the new Nathan Straus Library on 53rd Street has remained with me throughout my life. It was an Irish folktale, whose particulars escape me today, but at the end one character says to our central character something to the effect: "How did you get from there to here?" The answer was, "Why, by putting one foot in front of the other."

In the world of young adult library services it sometimes seems as though we are in the game where we can take one step forward but two backward, but for me, the scene was set for an amazing journey in librarianship.

My first assignment was at the 86th Street Branch Library and we had a very big problem: someone was stealing the *Encyclopaedia Britannica,* volume by volume. Working in the Reference Room of the library was like being an undercover FBI agent. I can't remember who eventually identified the man, but the police did make an arrest. The man was selling the encyclopedia volume by volume, whether for food or drugs, we never knew.

The New York Public Library closed the branch for rehabilitation and I was shipped off to the Countee Cullen Branch, which, to this day, remains one of my happiest work experiences. I wish I could remember the branch librarian's name because she was a hoot. If we didn't hang our coats up (there was space for them), she'd confiscate them and when it came time to go home, we were often in big trouble.

Coffee-break time at Countee Cullen was an *event!* One of the staff members took orders for coffee and Danish and went across the street to this small restaurant and then we gathered in two shifts to share our morning sustenance. When it came time for me to go for the coffee and Danish, a second librarian was assigned to go with me. My nose was a little out of joint by that, feeling as I did that I was capable of the task. Only on my next trip, when I went alone, did I learn why I had had a companion. Two very large black men were at the counter when I entered, and one looked at the woman owner taking my order and said, "What's that white girl doing here?" The owner replied, "You shut your mouth. She's with the library!" I can truthfully tell you that it was only at that moment that I realized I was the only white person on the staff. I also learned why even in the worst of the Harlem riots, the Countee Cullen Library never experienced so much as a broken window. It was an icon, and deservedly so.

A lesson I learned from working there was that no book collection can be selected for a branch by a central office. Everyone downtown was totally enamored with the Mary Stolz books and as a good apprentice, I set myself the task of reading them. I was barely into the first one when I found I had to cut the pages apart. The book had been checked out a dozen times, but no one in our neighborhood had actually read it.

One of the most important lessons I learned was to trust my instincts when it came to working with adolescents. We had a regular clientele, not many readers, but good sociable young people. One young man never took his cap off. In those days we were supposed to enforce acceptable manners as well as do library work, but something told me not to make an issue of his cap and I didn't.

Then came the night when we closed up the library and I found six or seven of the young men waiting on the steps. One said, casually, "We're going to walk you to the subway." I said something like "You don't have to but it's nice of you to do it." Only later did I learn that the rumor was out that there was going to be big trouble that night and the young men wanted to be sure their white librarian didn't get caught in the middle.

Some time later, when I learned why I'd had an escort, I asked one of the young men why they had been so good as to do that for me. He said, " 'Cause you don't hassle Lamar about his hat. You see, he's got red hair and he don't like anyone seeing it and making fun of him."

I could have happily spent the rest of my life at Countee Cullen, but they closed it for rehabilitation. If that sounds like a pattern, remember that all through the Depression and World War II there weren't funds for building maintenance and the affluent 1950s were finally allowing public sector agencies to do needed repairs.

Before I went to my next branch, Margaret Scoggin called me into her office and said, in effect, "I am asking you to go to X Branch (also in Harlem) but I will not order you to do so. The branch librarian is a major problem and she will not let the new young adult books reach the shelves until she has looked at each and every one of them, and they have been piling up for months in her office. If you can get her to release some of the books, it will be a great service to the young people using the branch.

If you decide to go, I want you to understand that you only have to stay as long as you can stand it. Please tell me when it becomes too much for you."

Wow! I would not only give it a try, I would have walked over hot coals for Margaret Scoggin. Any boss that upfront about a situation inspires enduring loyalty. It was even more amazing coming from Scoggin, whose public persona was of a very remote, private person. I doubt that anyone ever thought of her as a mother figure.

To say that the branch librarian was a major problem was an understatement. It was rumored that she had twenty-five cats and her bathtub was their litter pan. (In those days, by the way, what we now call litter did not yet exist, so a litter pan consisted of torn up strips of newspaper.) Getting close to Miss M. gave credence to the rumor.

One of her many flaws was following staff members around, even when they went to the bathroom. She was a true nut case and to this day I don't remember what I might have said or done that led her to stand in her office doorway, which adjoined the Young Adult section, and throw book after book at me. They bounced off the table, landed on the floor, missed my head, but, by golly, we had some new books on the shelves.

The staff fought to be able to work the nights when Miss M. didn't, and I remember holding down the first floor fort one night when four young men dashed through the front door, pulled off jackets and hats, and each picked a book off the shelf and sat looking for all the world like ideal students. Within seconds, a policeman followed, bellowing about how long had they been here? I looked at the policeman, looked at the young men, and said in a calm, but lying, voice, "All evening, officer." He glared and departed and so did the young men shortly thereafter.

To this day I cannot bring myself to feel guilty about that event. Almost every day the newspapers had stories about some kid being shot down for nothing more than kicking over a trash barrel and running from the police.

My next assignment took me to the Bronx Bookmobile, headquartered at the Mott Haven Branch. We had one of the bookmobiles whose entire side lifted up, and on nice weather days it was raised and we circulated books while standing on the sidewalk enjoying the sunshine and fresh air. It was a very nice way to earn a living.

It was on that assignment that I encountered the first black person who openly talked about hating white people, *all* white people. As we sat around the table having lunch, she would say things like, "If I had an atomic bomb, I'd drop it on white people." If one of us made the mistake of replying, "That's pretty silly. An atomic bomb would also kill a lot of black people." "Worth it," she'd reply. The situation never got out of hand because our supervisor, Naomi Noyes, made it clear by her demeanor that we were not to be baited into a confrontation. Learning that a person can be hated just for "*being one of them*" was vital to my personal growth and heavily influenced my thought patterns from that point on, including my choice of topic for a doctoral dissertation.

While my time at the New York Public Library was all too brief (I did get that M.L.S.), it was filled with memorable events. But the New York Public Library was not perfect; no organization ever is. One of my very first classes at Columbia was with Frances Henne, who was the visiting professor from the University of Chicago who never left Columbia until her retirement. I will always remember that first session when this portly woman with the dry Midwest accent walked through the door. Within fifteen minutes I was in love. It's hard to be absolutely smitten with someone and discover that at work you'd better keep it to yourself. The public librarians in the New York City area were *not* Frances Henne fans in those days.

It took a number of years for me to unravel the reasons for the coolness toward this great woman. In the old days, an Executive Secretary at ALA was paid not on a standard scale but by the number of members a division had. The ALA members, who were children's, young adult, and school librarians, were all under one Executive Secretary named Mildred Batchelder until the school people formed their own division, thus costing Batchelder her salary. Although it happened after Henne had been president of the school section, it was generally felt among the public librarians that she was to blame for the situation. Later in life she told me she really had nothing to do with it, that no one has less power than a past-president, but the perception of Frances as the leader carried over to that situation.

In retrospect, what is so strange about that situation is that there was a total absence of emphasis on professional association participation in any of our meetings. No one ever reported having gone to the New York Library Association or American Library Association conferences and what happened at either meeting. There was a parochial attitude that made NYPL the center of the library universe and participation in professional activities received short shrift. It is a joy today to see that young adult specialists from NYPL are serving on important YALSA committees and participating in all phases of professional activities. Both they and we benefit from our differing perspectives.

It is also important for current librarians to understand that there was a great deal of self-censorship practiced by even the biggest libraries. I remember being told that Hemingway's *Old Man and the Sea* was not put on *Books for the Teen Age* because recommending it might lead young people to want to read some of his other books, which were deemed inappropriate for that age group.

I also remember seeing an in-house review of a book that said it was not recommended and to see page X for the reason. On page X one character told another to "Go fuck yourself," to which the second character replied something to the effect that it was anatomically impossible. That exchange was enough to remove the book from consideration.

Having said all this, let me reiterate, I do not regret one single moment of working with and for some of the major pioneers in work with young adults. Their dedication to the age group was a defining moment for my professional development.

Encountering the Great Margaret Edwards

I never really "knew" Margaret Edwards. My personal contacts with her consisted solely of sitting in her farmhouse once with Mary K. Chelton as we had a fairly innocuous visit and one encounter, another time, in an exhibit booth at an ALA conference.

During most of the 1960s, I wrote a regular column for *School Library Journal*. In one of those columns I suggested that since librarians could not possibly reach all the young people in a community, they should work closely with other youth workers to see that they and the children and adolescents they worked with understood what the library could offer both groups. I believed then, and still do, that networking with other youth workers is a vital function for youth services librarians.

At the conference I was doing what I always did and still do: browsing the exhibits to see what books would be forthcoming in the fall from the publishers. Without so much as a hello or even identifying herself, this woman accosted me, correctly identifying me from my registration badge as *the* infamous Dorothy Broderick. That person was Margaret Edwards and she launched into an attack on the entire concept of networking: we were reader's advisers and that was that. Our purpose was to get the young people who came into the library to read good books. End of discussion.

From early in my life, I've had strong opinions on just about everything that crosses my mental path, but the seeming arrogance of Edwards completely overwhelmed me. It appeared to me that an idea foreign to her was not deemed worthy of discussing.

That encounter shed considerable light on the problem of a co-worker I had met a decade earlier while working as a children's librarian on Long Island. She had been badly scarred by having gone through the Enoch Pratt training for young adult librarians and being found unworthy. Since she was an excellent librarian, I could not understand at the time why she was so low in self-esteem because one librarian somewhere had judged her wanting. After my run-in, I had a better idea why my friend felt as she did.

In February 1994, *Voice of Youth Advocates* published an article called "Reading in a Not-So-Perfect World" by Carole A. Barham. In it, Barham states she doesn't do booktalks because she was humiliated by "a well-known expert on YA literature" in a course at Rutgers during the summer of 1974. That expert was Margaret Edwards.

To be fair, some of the very best librarians I've ever known attribute their success to Edwards's training. She believed that every librarian should be a top notch public speaker and the extroverts took to that concept with great enthusiasm. Booktalking came naturally to them and they relished being on stage. They have become national leaders in the field and have inspired many others to be better than they thought they could be.

Whether producing those stars justifies the harsh treatment of others, I leave to each person to decide.

Two Pioneers of Young Adult Library Services

1

Mary K. Chelton Interviews
Mabel Williams

E very profession should remember its beginnings, the origins of its ideals and the difficulties and circumstances of their forging. The innovators and pioneers who were there at the start should be respected and commemorated, even as we continue to reevaluate their legacy to make it relevant for our own times. As young adult librarians we revere the charismatic and strong-minded Margaret Edwards, even naming our top award for her. But who can name any earlier pioneers of our calling, much less remember their accomplishments?

In 1975 Mary K. Chelton, Grolier Award winner and co-founder of *Voice of Youth Advocates* magazine, went in search of these roots. The trail led to a retirement home in Hightstown, New Jersey, where Chelton interviewed Mabel Williams, the very first official Young Adult Librarian. In 1914 the great children's librarian Anne Carroll Moore had plucked Williams out of a conference and summoned her to New York Public Library to give struc-

Anne Carroll Moore

ture to her conviction that there should be some way to keep older children from losing interest in the library as they grew up. Williams, in a career that spanned thirty-eight years, took that assignment and built it into a shape that has endured as our profession.

But Mabel Williams, whom Frances Clarke Sayers has called "that sane and humorous woman,"[1] lacked the flamboyance of Margaret Edwards and her skill with the pen, and so was almost forgotten by the time Chelton tracked her down in New Jersey. She was eighty-eight, still cheerfully at work among books, establishing a library in the retirement home. Five years later Chelton was to spearhead the campaign that led to Williams being given the Grolier Award, and a picture published in the *American Library Association Yearbook* at that time shows her as still bright-eyed at ninety-three, a slight woman with a pointed chin, wavy white hair, and heavy-rimmed glasses.[2]

On those two winter afternoons in 1975, when Chelton sat opposite Mabel Williams in a rocking chair in her little room crowded with the mementos of a lifetime, she was eager to reminisce. Although her memories had by that time become somewhat stylized and exact dates often escaped her, she remembered her colleagues from the early days with humor, often impaling them with a piquant phrase or two that brought these shadowy pioneers vividly into focus.

"I graduated from the Simmons College Library School in 1909 and my first job was at the Radcliffe College Library," she began. But this first job was a disappointment. As a new person in a college library, Williams "was not having contact with the students or books." Much to her annoyance, she was delegated to the back room to mend torn pages and bindings, a task that failed to draw on her considerable energy and idealism. She went back to Simmons and indignantly told them she wanted another job. Within six months they had found her one—at the Somerville, Massachusetts, Public Library, where they "were just about to move from the old building to the new. That was a wonderful experience for me!" she recalled, smiling. Relishing the excitement of the new quarters, Williams was assigned to organize reference work in the adult department. "Then I was asked to go to the high school and introduce them to the reference work and to the regular reading for young people." It was this experience that brought her to the attention of Anne Carroll Moore in 1914.

Moore—or ACM, as her colleagues called her— was already a mighty force to be reckoned with in the profession. Eight years into her job as Director of Work with Children at the New York Public Library, she had been establishing branch children's rooms throughout the system at a furious pace with the newly available Carnegie Corporation of New York funds and was well on her way to making her office the mecca for children's librarians, writers, and editors from all over the world. The daughter of a Maine senator and the only girl among seven older brothers, Moore grew up with a strong and determined personality. Her biographer Frances Clarke Sayers praises her for her "high originality"[3] as well as "the strength of her belief in her own infallibility."[4] In 1895, at the age of twenty-four, she used these abilities to talk her way into the program of the Pratt Institute in New York City, although she had had no college experience. There she trained as a librarian and the next year was invited to develop the Institute's children's library—"at a time when education for librarianship was at its beginning and work with children seething to discover its definitive form and philosophy."[5] ACM was equal to the task, and in 1906 she was invited to become the New York Public Library's first Director of Work with Children.[6]

In the young Mabel Williams, Moore saw the person she was looking for to build a working relationship between the library and the city schools. "She came to a library meeting in Somerville," Williams remembered, "and I said something to her, and she wanted to have an interview with me. I had never met her. . . . When I got through the interview, she wanted to know if I were going to stay in New England all my life. She herself was a New Englander, so I realized she was playing on her own experience. So I said I hadn't thought about it. And she said, 'Well, if you decide that you're interested, write to me.' "

Williams stayed cool, in spite of this surprising offer. "I went home and talked to my parents. I was an only child and they didn't want me to go away from home. My father did, but my mother didn't. And we decided that I would go. So I wrote to Miss Moore, and right away, almost the next day, I got a letter telling me to come. And so I went there and I lived up in Columbia where all those various people do live who are in that kind of work, and she started me in the children's room. . . . I didn't know what was in the back of her mind for the future, until she told me, after she had tried me out as a children's librarian."

At first Williams worked in the second-floor children's room of one of the new branches. "I'd never been in a big city, or in these big libraries which were built under the Carnegie grants." The young New Englander was startled and amused by her first contacts with New York's teeming millions. "It was a time when immigration was very heavy and all the branch libraries in New York were filled with these immigrant children. . . . One morning a girl came in—she couldn't have been more than twelve—and she had this infant on her shoulder, and I told her she had to sign her name to join the library. She said, 'Well, wait till I put my uncle down. . . .' Then the next thing that happened right after that was a child came in with a pair of scissors in her hands and I asked her what she was going to do with them, and she said, 'My teacher told me to get a picture for my composition.' I said, 'Well, she didn't tell you to come to the library for it, did she?' 'No, but it was the only place that I can get one. . . .' These were immigrant children, you see, and they had no background with the library. And of course I explained it and told her there were some magazines in the back room and I would try to get her something. And that was quite an experience to realize it was quite difficult for all those poor youngsters who had nothing in their homes.

"Miss Moore kept me in the children's room, I guess about six months, and then she took me into her office and I went from her office to the different libraries to study the adult departments." ACM had had difficulties with resistance from the branches to her plans for children's service: "Because for a long time the librarians were pretty elderly. They had no pensions, no way of leaving, and so they had to work." When the library instigated a retirement system a few years later, the picture changed immediately. But during this period the old ladies gave Williams a hard time in a way that will be familiar to many contemporary YA librarians. "They didn't like these youngsters coming in and they were just opposed to what I wanted to do."

But she continued to infiltrate the system, with ACM's backing. "Miss Moore really considered the work I was doing with schools. And we felt the best way to do it was have each branch canvas their whole district and go into those schools and invite them." Teachers were made welcome to bring their classes to the library or, failing that, were encouraged to invite librarians to visit the schoolroom. Soon ACM revealed her further agenda. "And then Miss Moore wanted to have an adult department for young people, because she didn't want to lose these children from the Children's Room, have them drop the public library entirely, and after I'd been there quite a while she asked me to develop that department. It was work with young adults, and it was about 1919."

Mabel Williams was given a title—Supervisor of Work with Schools—and took her place as one of three "assistants" under ACM, the Director of Work with Children. The other two were the Supervisor of

Work with Children in the Extension Division—the "traveling libraries"—and the Supervisor of Storytelling. This last position was at the time held by the dramatic Anna Cogswell Tyler, who had succeeded ACM at Pratt Institute and had later joined her at NYPL to develop storytelling into an art.

Williams and Tyler shared space in Anne Carroll Moore's office, the famous Room 105 at the Forty-Second Street Central Library. Frances Clarke Sayers, in her biography of Anne Carroll Moore, has described the excitement of that book-lined room whose "influence . . . was to reach out literally across the world.[7] . . . Any efficiency engineer studying the flow of traffic in Room 105 would have suffered a nervous breakdown."[8] "A cluster of small desks like so many ducklings in a crowded nest stood in front of the east wall, and here was 'the office' of the Supervisor of Storytelling, 'the office' of the first assistant, a junior assistant, and 'the office' of the Supervisor of Work with Schools until 1924. . . . Into that room came trooping on a monthly schedule, the children's librarians . . . for . . . a time of private conference and discussion with ACM." Other regular visitors were children's writers, illustrators, and publishers, as well as librarians from all over the world. Only one phone served this busy office, and for ACM it meant that "every time the telephone summoned her it entailed a scramble from behind the entanglements of her desk . . . a stumble around the chair where the interviewees sat, into the clear space before the table where ACM conducted her affairs in full view of people passing down the corridor and in full sound of an office staff adept at working at their separate tasks as if theirs was an ordinary office instead of the focal point of a disciplined, fascinating, and often joyous world in which one had to be prepared for 'no end of surprises.' "[9]

From this chaotic office Williams began to build her service to young people. Her first objective was to recruit sympathetic staff throughout the system. "I went to every branch. I went all over . . . I had meetings, you see, and I'd try to get a representative from each branch or try to find someone who was interested in doing it." Her conciliatory approach was a marked contrast to the methods of ACM, who had begun her campaign for personnel in the branches by staking out the territory with a job title and a salary grade for children's librarians—a contrast in style between the two specialties that has continued to undercut the stature of young adult services.

Just when it was needed, a creative solution to finding enthusiastic young adult librarians emerged. "Miss Oberton, who was the head of placement, . . . suggested that graduates of a college might . . . want to try library work with no training.

And so she suggested that we take them in at a lower salary and put them around in these rooms for training and then if they wanted to take their year of library service, they could do that. And many of them did. They really were a wonderful group. . . . You got very different people that way, and I'll never forget them. . . . And then, of course, we had other people . . . in the system who wanted to try it." One of these "other people" was Lillian Morrison, who was to become the head of young adult services herself in 1968. "She was a cataloguer. . . . And she hated it. And so . . . Miss Oberton sent her to me. Well, she hardly waited for me to stop talking and she said she wanted to do it. . . . She was a wonderful worker.

"I was allowed gradually to appoint a librarian in each adult department of the branch library to give full time to that work. That was difficult to get at first, but we finally achieved it. And when they had that position, their job was to go out to the schools in the neighborhood and make the contacts, and if possible, bring the teachers and the class into the library. . . . And so usually we took them into the adult room, showed them around and gave them something to look up in the catalog, so they wouldn't feel they were leaving that building for-ever." At first, the idea was to ease the transition from the children's room to the adult library, and so the visiting classes were usually eighth- and ninth-graders who had reached the end of children's service and were ready to begin high school or go out into the world of work. "We always tried to take the last grade in the school and have them come into the library. And we took them into the adult department, because it was downstairs. And they were each given a card to find a book, so they'd get a little feeling about it. Every graduating class had that experience."

But almost at once, she broke out of that narrow concept of library service to youth. "From Mabel Williams's vision," says Frances Clarke Sayers, ". . . the distinctive work with young people was to emerge with comparable space and service in branch libraries for children in their teens as was sustained on behalf of children in the elementary grades. And here also guns were fired in continuous salvos of salute honoring individual reading, spontaneously pursued. . . ."[10] By 1924 Williams had her own office on the third floor in the Fifty-eighth Street Branch, which had been chosen because it was near the Board of Education. "And there," she recalled, "I had a teachers' conference room and it was also a room to administer this adult department, to work with the books for young people."

And a room to train librarians in this new craft. When classes couldn't come to the library, "we built up this book talk and worked with the schools, going in taking an armful of books with us and introducing them in the classes." Williams soon found that her staff needed to learn and practice booktalking and to discuss books together. "I had to have meetings," she decided. Three or four people in the children's department offered to help in teaching skills, among them Mary Gould Davis, who in 1923 had replaced Anna Cogswell Tyler as Supervisor of Storytelling.[11] "We formed a book committee, because she was interested in this older group just as well as the younger. . . . We decided the thing to do was to assign people to give talks at different meetings. You know what that would be like! At first, they were a little skittish about it, but we had wonderful times, especially with Miss Davis, who, of course, loved doing it and helped tremendously. . . . They discussed the books, and then they went back and worked with the books." Much to Williams's trepidation, Anne Carroll Moore regularly came to these meetings. "I thought that was dreadful at first, but I found she wasn't going to be critical, in fact, and enjoyed it. She just came."

At this point, Mary K. Chelton could not resist asking a provocative question about Williams's relationship with the legendary Anne Carroll Moore. "What was she like? What is your memory of her?" With characteristic self-effacement, Williams gave

Mabel Williams

ACM her due, both as to her genius and the difficulties of working closely with such a strong personality. "She was a wonderful person. Of course she was the one who started me off, and until the very end she was interested in what I was doing. . . . I don't think I ever would have been active in anything if she hadn't given me a big push." She recalled wryly the first annual report she filed for ACM. "She made me write it over again. Because she said it was too technical, it didn't have any heart in it. . . . She didn't like people who were too organized. She liked people who had originality, I suppose. That's what she was always looking for."

"Did she ever have problems with the kinds of original thinkers she picked? With them disliking each other?" Chelton ventured. "Yes," Williams nodded. "She would have nothing to do with some of them. She'd throw them out. . . . Oh yes, she was the one who had very definite ideas and stuck by them!" But, without rancor, she added, "I get on with people like that, but it means that I'm not as determined as they are. I have to fit in." ("Somebody has to compromise," muttered Chelton darkly.) "That's right," Williams agreed sunnily. "I was very fond of her and I never had any rows at all. She was amazing."

Chelton pushed further. "Was she personally interested in the young adult age group?" Williams

responded quickly, giving generous credit. "Yes,
she was, because she felt that all her work was lost
if they just dropped. She was the one who thought
of it, because I don't think anyone else had thought
of having a special work of that kind. . . . I think she
was chiefly interested in getting them into the adult
department. That's what she was working on and
what I was supposed to accomplish."

But Mabel Williams continued to develop her
own concepts of service to young people. "I began
at the very beginning to make contact with the high
schools, because that was my main objective," she
affirmed, although her assignment as Supervisor of
Work with Schools included all ages. Spanning the
whole range of grades from kindergarten through
high school she found "very stimulating. . . . I felt I
had to do some of that in order to know the whole
picture. I don't say I really knew it as deeply as you
have to do, but I think that I did tie them up somewhat, so there was a good feeling there. . . . I had a
very nice relationship with all the children's librarians."

At the same time she was creating a browsing collection for teenagers in the central library's adult
area, chosen from adult books (because, of course,
there were then almost no books especially written
for this age), and also assembling a staff with an understanding of adolescents. "It was a little difficult

until we got some people on the floor there to limber up things a bit. When we finally got the adult department, we had a special section where we had books for them, and someone there all the time to meet them. . . . Of course, we encouraged them to use the whole thing, but we had to have something to start with. . . . As time went on, the branch librarians were very helpful."

The need for lists of books to help the librarians in this service very soon became apparent. At first, they were informal typewritten pages. But in 1929 Williams and her staff put together the first annual compilation of "Books for Young People," which was to become "Books for the Teen Age," that dependable mainstay of YA librarians. From the first, the selection of books for the list was a group endeavor. "Sometimes we gave them to certain young people to read. But it just grew. We had other people's lists, and, of course, in order to introduce a book we had to read it. . . . perhaps somebody recommended them. . . . We had to do a lot of reading. . . . And that's the way we did up the list, each one speaking of the one they'd enjoyed. . . . Every year we approved this list, you see. We worked through the year and these meetings we had were preparing for that list."

Censorship was not a problem for the sensible Mabel Williams. "Of course, we used a great many of the books for older people in the children's room, and they were very carefully selected. . . . I didn't screen out anything, but I didn't put in certain things. I think I was more particular in the beginning; then, when I got to know the young people and some of the teachers, I limbered up a little. I was always trying to feel what the teachers' reactions to books were."

But there were many teenagers who never got to high school. Thousands were leaving school to go to work right after eighth grade. To meet the growing concern about the truncated educations of these youths, continuation schools were established, and the New York Public Library appointed a Vocational Schools Specialist. Margaret Scoggin initiated this work[12] but was soon succeeded by the charismatic Amelia Munson.

Williams remembered her vividly: "She was a teacher. She'd never had anything to do with libraries. And she was a person who had her own opinions and would make her way. . . . Well, she came to New York. She lived upstate somewhere . . . she was a regular country girl. But she had read it all . . . the poets, she knew them and she was crazy about Robert Frost. . . . I think she picked out our department because she wanted to do the work with books and there wasn't really any other that was doing it."

Wisely, Williams let Munson shape the job

around her extraordinary talents. "We all knew her ability and I don't think she was given a special title of any kind. She was just a member of the work with young people but she worked with older people, too. . . . I guess she really considered herself my assistant, but she was on her own really, and very busy with her own things she could do. I just gave her her head, because that's the way you have to work with a person like that. . . . She made people think. . . . She didn't care too much about what happened as a result." ("Impetuous," suggested Chelton.) "Yes. I'm fascinated by these things flying up in the air," confessed Williams, waving her arms toward the ceiling. "Gracious!" She was silent a moment, remembering Munson. "She had great knowledge and ability to present poetry and so we all would just sit spellbound listening to anything she recited or talked about. . . . She could just recite reams of poetry and send tears down your cheeks." Munson was in great demand for performances at school assemblies. "She had quite a lot of special requests. . . . I used to go to assemblies when I was asked to, but as time went on, I had experts that I thought were better. I'd send Miss Munson. They'd want the special things. And Lilly [Morrison] got quite a reputation for that, . . . especially in the high schools."

But Amelia Munson also focused her energies on

the more mundane aspects of her job. In 1927 her paper "Library Service to Employed Youth" was read at the Conference on Education of Employed Youth in New York City and was widely reprinted.[13] She continued to write for the library press, and in 1950 the American Library Association published her book *An Ample Field*, the first comprehensive statement of the ideals of the new specialty of young adult librarianship.

Another giant-sized talent nurtured by Mabel Williams was Margaret Scoggin, who eventually became her successor in 1952. "Her background was in classical studies, . . . but she didn't use it much after she started what we were doing." Scoggin had gone to school in England and "never did take the state library school in this country." After her beginning assignment with the vocational schools, she was soon chosen to develop the newly funded Nathan Straus Branch for Children and Young People. "There was a branch way down in the Forties over on the West Side and it wasn't used very much." The philanthropist Nathan Straus left money to the library for a designated purpose: "In the will, it said that he wanted it to keep young people off the streets, and the lawyers said that they had to build a special place for young people, because it was in the will, so we got it without any effort." Margaret Scoggin set to with gusto. "We sent her over there

. . . and that's the way she liked to work. She and Mr. Harper, the head of the circulation department, did all the planning of the building. . . . Oh, she had a wonderful time! She went to town, and he [Straus] paid for it, I suppose."

Margaret Scoggin's Nathan Straus Branch became the young adult equivalent of Anne Carroll Moore's central children's room. "They had wonderful meetings there," remembered Williams. "Pearl Buck . . . loved to come . . . evenings and talk to young people. And it got to be sort of a hangout, with those young people. . . . It was very successful. . . . And then she had a regular staff and, of course, Miss Morrison was with her. These people who came along and were so good seemed to take from each other. . . . And, of course, that Nathan Straus Branch was a wonderful training ground for all the people who worked there with Miss Scoggin. It was a wonderful picture of work with young people."

Scoggin not only excelled in creative library service and programming—even organizing a radio program of teen book reviews—but she also brought a keen interest to the selection of books for teens. From 1935 to 1946 she contributed an annual list of suitable titles to *Library Journal*. At first, it was called "Books for Older Boys and Girls,"[14] but in 1944 Scoggin began to use the term that has become standard when she switched to "Books for Young

Adults."[15] (The earliest documented use of that phrase seems to be about 1937).[16] Because she retired in 1968, she was never to experience the joy of working with serious young adult literature, but she foreshadowed its coming in 1953 in "Outlook Tower," the column of book review she wrote for many years for *Horn Book*: "Our authors are experimenting. Their task is to bring the 'junior novel' closer to the good adult novel in style, characterization, and human understanding. More power to them!"[17]

Mabel Williams recalled other figures from her past: Miss Bayard, who was doing a similar job at the Brooklyn Public Library—"She used to come over and talk things over with me . . . sometimes she would come to one of our meetings"—and Anne Izard, who worked briefly as a junior assistant in ACM's department and later became the children's consultant at the Westchester Library System in Mount Vernon, New York (where Mary K. Chelton knew her), a president of the Children's Services Division of the American Library Association, and a Grolier winner.

But the most charismatic of all was Margaret Edwards, who made a historic visit to Mabel Williams's terrain in the mid-thirties. In an interview with Mary K. Chelton much later, Edwards recalled Williams's kindness and influence: "Though I was unknown and an amateur in the field, she took me under her wing and showed me everything that might help me. As we rode from place to place, she discussed ideas and philosophy of the work with me. . . . I talked to branch staffs, visited Margaret Scoggin's branch, and learned and learned."[18] Mabel Williams, too, remembered the visit with pleasure. "I had my car then and we drove around the city. She was very, very amusing."

And also very, very opinionated: "She was very critical of everything in the library. I don't know that she was unkind about it, but there were a lot of things that she thought needed changing." She was particularly disapproving of a branch where "juvenile delinquency was a problem" and the librarians had enticed the young adults into the library with checker boards and other board games. "This was the one activity I observed that I could not accept" Margaret Edwards told Chelton. "I may be wrong, but I've always felt that fun and games and entertainment as ends in themselves are not justified in the library. I know many young librarians who would disagree, but I sometimes think we go far afield to avoid the hard work and creativity necessary to make reading appealing."[19]

Nor was programming particularly part of Williams's philosophy of YA library service, unless it fell into her lap. Yet she did remember one or two grand occasions for young adults at the Central Library. "A Mrs. Ames, who was very wealthy . . . went to the head department in the library and said she would like to get a group of good college material in the high schools" together to hear the writer Santha Rama Rau speak. "So Mr. Harper [the head of circulation to whom Williams reported] came to me and said, 'What are you going to do about that?' I said, 'Well, I'll go to the heads of the English departments and ask for each one to pick out a certain number who would appreciate it.' "

The chosen ones from all over the city assembled on the big night, and Santha Rama Rau "came dressed in this sari—Oh, she was stunning! And, of course, these girls were just spellbound, and she gave a wonderful talk about her home and about how she'd come to America to college and all that. It was very, very successful . . . and it was nice because it brought all the high schools together. . . . And I think English departments all over the city became more aware when they picked out the brightest ones.

"And then another time . . . one of the wealthy people wanted Mr. [Guthrie] McClintic, the actor . . . (His wife was Katherine Cornell). . . . It was the same woman, and she wanted me to get a group together and have him read a play for them. So I did the same thing. And before the play began, he came to me and said, 'You know, I'm scared to death. I've never had anything to do with high school children and I had to do this because she's a friend of mine,' and I said, 'Well, don't you be afraid; they will be spellbound,' and you just could hear a pin drop. And when it was over he came back very much pleased."

Usually she left such productions to Margaret Scoggin at the Nathan Straus Branch, where the schedule of speakers, book groups, and discussions rivaled the brilliant parade of talent at Anne Carroll Moore's central children's room, or to Anna Cogswell Tyler or, later, Mary Gould Davis, whose dramatic storytelling sessions often included book clubs for young readers. Williams contented herself with building a steady, solid structure of book-grounded YA work. Chelton attempted to sum it up: "If I'm hearing you right, it sounds as if the program were a very well-trained staff and very book-oriented so that they did very good individual readers' advisory work and very good booktalk work, mostly with school groups that came to the library or they went out." Mabel Williams nodded emphatically. "That's it."

As the older woman grew visibly tired, Chelton hurried to sum up a few more details. The budget problem during the Depression? "I don't think I had anything to do with that. I probably begged for books. Miss Moore—that was her sacred position, handling the ordering and all that sort of thing." The role of men in Mabel Williams library world? "There weren't very many, and I think they felt that they'd leave it to the women. They had their part and we had ours. . . . I don't remember any branch librarian that was a man." (Nor was any director of the New York Public Library ever a woman, Chelton reminded her.) Which of the many immigrant groups were predominant in using the library? "I think the Jewish, and, well, let's see, the Irish were the least, in a way, but they were fun. . . . they didn't take it too seriously. And Italians were pretty good. We had all the different languages."

In contrast to Anne Carroll Moore's active role in influencing the writers and publishers of children's books, Williams made no such attempts to steer the makers of literature for teens. "Why didn't you have a lot of publishers coming in?" asked Chelton. "Well, because I didn't feel I had the ability that she had," Williams answered with honest modesty. Nor was she interested in teaching or lecturing at colleges, as ACM and Scoggin did. "They were the ones who had the gift, I thought. . . . I never had that ambition. I wanted to remain with the people. I didn't want to give that up. . . . I had to go around and visit all these people who were doing the work. I would check up on them all the time." At the time of her retirement in 1952, her domain had grown to thirty-five branches or more, and she kept in close touch with all of them through constant visits and monthly meetings.

The face of sensible, down-to-earth Mabel Williams glowed as she watched Mary K. Chelton gather up the notes that summarized her life. "It was great fun," she said contentedly. "I enjoyed my work tremendously."

Notes

1. Frances Clarke Sayers. *Anne Carroll Moore: A Biography*. New York: New York, Atheneum, 1972, 199.
2. *American Library Association Yearbook 1981*. Chicago: ALA, 1981, 79.
3. Sayers, 121.
4. Sayers, 120.
5. Sayers, 62.
6. Sayers, 110.
7. Sayers, 204.
8. Ibid.
9. Sayers, 202.
10. Sayers, 200.
11. *Wilson Library Bulletin* (June 1956): 12.
12. *Top of the News* (November 1968: 68.
13. *Library Journal* (November 1, 1927): 1034.
14. See "Young People's Reading," in *Library Literature 1933*. New York: Wilson, 1936.

15. See "Young People's Work," in *Library Literature 1943–1945*. New York, Wilson, 1946.

16. See "Young People's Work," in *Library Literature 1936–1939*. New York: Wilson, 1941.

17. *Top of the News* (November 1968): 75.

18. Mary K. Chelton. "Margaret Edwards: An Interview," *Voice of Youth Advocates* (August 1987): 112–13.

19. Ibid.

2

Reconsidering Margaret Edwards: The Relevance of *The Fair Garden* for the Nineties

I n 1993 I was invited by the American Library Association to write an introduction, footnotes, and bibliographies for their new edition of the holy icon of young adult librarianship, *The Fair Garden and the Swarm of Beasts* by Margaret Alexander Edwards. Challenged by the assignment, I threw myself into researching Edwards and her times and interviewing librarians who had known her, and eventually produced a sixty-page introduction that described her influential career at Enoch Pratt Free Library and evaluated *The Fair Garden* in perspective against a background of changing times and changing ideas in librarianship. The following essay is the unpublished second half of that foreword.

This new edition of the classic of our profession

raises some challenging questions for young adult library specialists today. What does *The Fair Garden and the Swarm of Beasts*, first published in 1969, have to say to us in the 1990s? How much of the Edwards heritage is still golden, and how well has it been integrated into today's young adult services? How many of her ideas have been shuffled aside by changing times, and how much of her philosophy is based on universal and lasting inspiration? To understand the real value of Margaret Edwards's enduring contribution to the profession she helped to invent, we have to see her heritage in perspective against the background of contemporary ideas and practices, as they have evolved over the last twenty years.

Much of the Edwards legacy is still thoroughly valid: her demanding but effective training methods, her insistence on the specialness of the young adult librarian, her emphasis on youth advocacy, and, most of all, her commitment to the promotion of reading as a life-changing activity for young people. About these things she was supremely right, but about some other matters she was dead wrong.

Hard Times for Young Adult Services

In the sixties, when *The Fair Garden* was first published, YA library services had ridden the crest of the wave of enthusiasm and federal funding, but by the late 1970s the tide had begun to turn. "Young Adult library work has begun to show signs of relapse, of . . . decline in vigor and freshness of trends begun in the 1960s . . ." wrote Miriam Braverman.[1] As early as the late sixties, some administrators had begun to question "the huge amounts of money that were being poured into young adult service."[2] By 1976 interest was waning in programming, and projects involving outreach services were the first to go as a cost-saving measure.[3] Robert Wedgeworth, then the Executive Director of ALA, suggested that libraries might better focus on "young people who are ready to use our services," rather than beat the bushes to round up a few more.[4] The population wave of teenagers had passed on, but the number of YA librarians had increased to meet the earlier demand and now approached a surplus, as YA positions were being eliminated. To add to the troubles, an economic reversal, a reduction of federal funds,[5] and a less favorable political climate in Washington led to budget cuts and hiring freezes.[6] Libraries entered "an era of conservatism and accountability," "and it was time to get serious.[7]

Young adult librarians could at least justify their literature being taken seriously. In 1978 the magazine *Voice of Youth Advocates* was founded by Dorothy Broderick and Mary K. Chelton and soon became not only a focus for the profession and a place to share struggles and successes, but a substantial resource for reviews. As adolescent literature grew in quantity and quality, a body of critical writing developed around it: increased recognition in the pages of *School Library Journal, Top of the News* (now renamed *Journal of Youth Services in Libraries*), *Horn Book,* and "The Young Adult Perplex" column in the *Wilson Library Bulletin,* written by me from 1978 until 1988, and then by Cathi Dunn MacRae until the demise of the magazine in 1995. Twayne's *Young Adult Author Series,* begun in 1985, dignified the lives and work of YA writers with serious biocritical studies, and Ken Donelson and Alleen Pace Nilsen wrote the definitive textbook in the field, *Literature for Today's Young Adults.* In the 1990s YA professional resources proliferated as general library staff found themselves floundering to serve young adults without a specialist. Two of the best guides to contemporary YA services are *Bare Bones: Young Adult Services Tips for Public Library Generalists* by Mary K. Chelton and James M. Rosinia and the brilliant but expensive *Connecting Young Adults and Libraries* by Patrick Jones, a book that is diametrically opposed to Margaret Edwards's philosophy in theory but not always in practice.

"In the 1990s, the young adult specialist is a scarce resource," admits ALA.[8] A set of statistics that had librarians gnashing their teeth in frustration was revealed by a National Center for Education Statistics Survey Report in 1988. The study found that 25 percent of public library users are young adults, while 89 percent of public libraries do not have a young adult librarian.[9] "Would a business that could identify one-quarter of its customers as a particular market segment not respond to this group directly?" raged Patrick Jones.[10] And this while 55 percent of libraries indicate an increase in services to YAs [11] and library circulation has been rising steadily every year since 1981.[12] "We are still fighting the same fight," said Joan Atkinson, "to get young adult work recognized and established."[13] The battle would be familiar to Margaret Edwards. But as the end of the century approached, a rise in the population of young adults heralded a renaissance in library services to that age group.

The Edwards Legacy: The Training of Librarians

When Edwards was asked in an interview near the end of her life to name the accomplishments for which she wanted to be remembered, she rattled off "The training of assistants, the bookwagon, work with schools, *The Fair Garden and the Swarm of Beasts*. Take your choice."[14]

The training of assistants was indeed one of Edwards's most impressive achievements and a feat that would be impossible today, even if a teacher with such a forceful personality could be found. Joseph Wheeler and his successors granted her the time and the staff to carry out the massive training program, evidently over the bitter objections of branch librarians and some of the young assistants themselves. In *Fair Garden* she describes the strenuous reading assignments and the many individual conferences—and the stunned reaction of the librarians: "Some of the assistants were unhappy, to say the least, and some branch librarians thought it was pretty hard to ask innocent young librarians to read a lot of books."[15] But consider the expenditure of time involved: 300 books at, say, three hours each, plus an hour conference with Edwards after each ten books, equals 930 hours—most of it on the librarian's own time. Sara Siebert, who later became Edwards's successor, remembers "I read and read and read. I put everything else aside to read. Those who were not encumbered by families did better."[16] The interviews, too, were demanding, as Edwards probed not only for literary opinions but for a sense of how the book could contribute to the maturation of teenagers and how it might be presented to them on the library floor. Graduates of Edwards's training program referred to it as "MAE Boot Camp" and the chair by her desk as "the hot seat."[17]

And yet who can disagree that librarians should be well-read, even if they have to do it on their own time? Dorothy Broderick has said, "Librarians who don't read are guilty of hypocrisy and should not be paid."[18] Perhaps those who perceive their profession to be information specialists can dispense with this requirement, but for Edwards's vision of the librarian as a reading consultant and guide it was essential. Most librarians, of course, do read with joy, but to those in our time who feel that they should be paid for this extracurricular activity, she would undoubtedly point out brusquely that no other professional expects to limit the job to what can be accomplished in forty hours at the office. Young adult librarians, especially, have a need to keep up with the newest and best, as Edwards would agree. A recent YALSA publication phrases it in a more contemporary way: "Librarians must be acquainted with a wide variety of books and other resources in a broad range of interests and formats."[19]

Later, when she had made inroads into the schools, Edwards also trained assistants in booktalking—and with no gentle hand. Sara Siebert recalls that the former Latin teacher once said to her, "Sit down. You're not really prepared for this," and then called on someone else to show how it was done. ("But for good reason," admits Siebert. "I was not prepared and only had 'played around' with the talk.") The Munder Room, a small conference room in the Pratt Library that was used for practicing booktalks, is recalled by Mary K. Chelton as "The Murder Room." "The acoustics were dreadful so you never knew how loud or soft it was unless they told you," says Chelton. Edwards would send the quaking YA assistant to the front of the room and then "she'd sit way in the back and criticize."[20]

To fill the many hours it took to visit every classroom in the school system, it was necessary for every YA librarian to be an active booktalker. Even those who were painfully shy of public speaking were expected to overcome their deficiencies. Siebert, who, because of a bad heart, had been excused from oral reports all through school, remembers that after her first booktalk she had constant indigestion which was diagnosed by an internist as "nerves." Later, as a library school teacher and workshop leader, Edwards used the same strict methods to put students through practical exercises.

Harsh as these stories sound, all those who survived her training praise her unstintingly with gratitude and affection (although she would probably be the first to point out that we have not heard from those who failed). "If you stuck to it, you soon learned that what she did was right. There was no question about it at all," says Siebert. "She was always trying to get you to be better than you were. She would not accept lesser than best." Linda Lapides, who served many years later as Siebert's second-in-command, agrees: "Margaret Edwards was such a big person, you knew she wasn't criticizing *you!*"[21] With memories from a later period, *Booklist* editor Sally Estes says, "Everyone adored her. You really felt that she wanted you to do good, that she was backing you, and that she was trying to teach you the right way. It was all constructive hardness. You felt good with her criticism. And she gave praise when praise was due."[22] Mary K. Chelton is more equivocal: "She was very precise about what she wanted you to know, and she was extremely explicit about her philosophy. She tended to seem autocratic to people who needed more room," but to the unsophisticated young Chelton, "It was sort of like listening to God speak. It was only later when I had to think about training people myself, that I realized how dysfunctional [her methods] could be for certain people."

But Anna Curry testifies that the booktalking skills she learned from Edwards helped her throughout her career: "Long after I left young adult work, I drew upon the public speaking techniques she taught. I used them with success in bud-

get appeals before the city council, before
community groups protesting threatened branch
closures, and testifying on Capitol Hill urging federal support for LSCA. Actually, in contrast to giving booktalks to urban high school students who
seldom disguised how boring they expected the
talks to be, some of the public speaking I did as Library Director offered hardly any challenge at all."[23]

It must be admitted that Edwards's methods
worked. She turned out confident and effective
working librarians and inspired many of them to
become leaders in the field. Such an ambitious training program in a public library now seems to us to
be the wildest luxury, as we struggle simply to keep
the doors open. But there is much to be learned
from Edwards's example and from the model of a
public library system that recognized the central importance of service to young people and gave top
priority to it. As YALSA's *Directions for Library Services to Young Adults* booklet says wistfully, "Administrators must ensure an ongoing program of staff
development."[24] Library schools, too, could ponder
Edwards's results and perhaps begin to grasp the
demonstrated fact that public librarians are not only
professionals who need a background in theory and
principles but are also missionaries who need clear
goals and performers who need to rehearse.

The Edwards Legacy:
The Specialness of YA Librarians

As she taught, Margaret Edwards had a clear vision before her of the ideal young adult librarian, and she was very sure that that person, rather than materials, was the key to good library service. "The young adult librarian must be an artist. He must have the original passion or capacity for feeling that any artist has. Then, he must learn how to perform—the technique to make his work effective," she wrote in *Fair Garden*.[25] This vision of the YA librarian as a special person has come down to us intact. In an interview with Mary K. Chelton, Edwards listed the qualities that define the breed. The young adult librarian, she said, "must be perfectly honest, with no pretenses, must read widely and constantly, must like young people . . . must strive for respect rather than love, and must have a sense of humor strong enough to laugh at himself"—all qualities embodied superbly in Edwards herself.[26]

She was scornful of the idea that any staff member, regardless of training or affinity for young people, can work with teens. But that situation has become today's uncomfortable reality. As Patrick Jones says, "It is clear that YA services are best with YA staff, but it is still the generalists who serve this special population."²⁷ If a library recognizes the importance of youth services, in some ways it may be beneficial for all staff to feel a responsibility to teens, even when there is a YA librarian on board. Edwards—who did battle with the "old biddies"—recognized the need to convert other staff to youth advocacy. A recent Public Library Association booklet even maintains that for staff to refer all teens to the YA specialist "isolates teens *and* the YA specialist from the library mainstream."²⁸

And isolation is a persistent state for contemporary young adult librarians, to a degree that would be inconceivable to those who shared the support and camaraderie of Pratt under Edwards and, later, Siebert. "One of the things that makes YA service difficult is a constant feeling of being under attack," says Patrick Jones.²⁹ The lack of advancement opportunities within YA were acknowledged grimly by Edwards and are still with us. In *Fair Garden* she lamented the tendency to promote good young adult librarians out of the specialty by making them branch librarians. "The only way up is in administering the system. Influencing young people to read and think has a limited future in the public library."³⁰ In 1993 a YALSA publication made the identical point: "Limited opportunities for advancement and inadequate recognition of achievement force many young adult specialists to seek administrative posts, which essentially promotes them out of young adult librarianship. There is a need for improved career ladders and compensation that encourages experienced specialists to stay in young adult work."[31]

The Edwards Legacy: Youth Advocacy

In the beginning of her career, Edwards felt that some of her colleagues saw her as a sort of police person assigned to work with teenagers to keep them out of other staff members' hair, an attitude that is still voiced as "What are we going to do with all these kids?"[32] The library in many cases continues to see young adults as an annoyance and an interruption. Whether they should be treated as a special group is an ongoing controversy among administrators,[33] as much as it was in Edwards's day when she harrumphed at libraries who bragged that they treated "'young people just like they do adults.' This means ignoring them completely unless they ask for information."[34] And sometimes, in our day as well as hers, staff attitudes go beyond indifference to hostility and dislike. As Dorothy Broderick, master of the pithy observance, has said: "I get awfully tired of adults who treat young people as dirt, [and] . . . complain about the lack of respect they receive from the young. Respect is a reciprocal action—give it and you get it."[35] Margaret Edwards knew this truth well and carried it on to a warm sympathy for her young patrons: "The soundest approach to the adolescent is to treat him as though he were a reasonable, dignified, mature person."[36] Her enjoyment of teenagers is echoed today by Patrick Jones when he writes, "the best thing about being a YA librarian is getting paid to sit and talk with and listen to YAs."[37]

Youth participation is an article of faith with contemporary YA librarians. "Young adults should be involved in the decision-making process in libraries. . . . From this, they learn responsibility, self-esteem, and confidence. They appreciate libraries more and have positive attitudes toward the library and its staff," says YALSA's *Directions for Library Services for Young Adults*.[38] We think of this as a recent development, so it is interesting to find in Edwards an early advocate for youth involvement. Although she never formed a YA Advisory Board, Pratt's book review publication *You're the Critic* was guided by a rotating board of students from each high school in the city. Her very first branch collections were based on the votes of teenage patrons. The "Teenage Testimony" project polled all ninth- through twelfth-grade students in the city to learn the titles of their favorite books and then advertised the results with a publication and an exhibition.[39] When she was faced with possible controversy over Felsen's *Two on the Town*, she sought opinions from a number of teens before defending the book. She advised librarians to ask constantly for reactions and spoke of her encounters with young adults as "that enriching experience." "Edwards's work formed the basis of youth advocacy in libraries," says Deborah Taylor, coordinator of School and Student Services at the Pratt Library. "It began in her work with promoting reading and providing access to young adult readers and evolved into an advocacy that includes all aspects of librarianship."[40]

At the small religious college where she studied to be a Latin teacher, it is unlikely that Edwards was exposed to formal training in the psychological dynamics of adolescence (although in later years she was adamant about the necessity for psychology courses in library schools).[41] Her orientation was literary rather than developmental, and the concept of a detailed progression of social and emotional tasks to be accomplished by the developing adolescent was not part of her perception. She focused on the young adult as he or she was to become if properly guided. The goal was always to create citizens of the world. Nowadays, we are more likely to stress personal and psychological growth, which Edwards saw as only the first step. The young reader was to be drawn out by the vicarious experience of reading through a series of concentric circles of concern, from concern for self to concern for family, community, city, country, and, finally, the world.

Edwards's young patrons in the forties and fifties lived in a simpler, less stressful world than today's teens do, and they were a different breed, "the eager, anxious understudies of adults."[42] Even the rebellious youths of the sixties won her support with their "eagerness to take up causes and protest, their readiness to overthrow the established order."[43] In later days she spoke prophetically of "the children of both the ghetto and suburbia . . . living in a world growing constantly smaller, of which they have very little understanding."[44]

Each decade has seen different kinds of teenagers and teenage problems and these changes are mirrored by changes in YA services. In our complex and dangerous world many young adults are now "at risk" from suicide, AIDS, pregnancy, unemployment, and gang violence. They have far less access to adults because of divorce, mobility, and the conflicting commitments of adult lives.[45] In addition, the youth population is more diverse today. All this makes expert and empathetic library service to them even more imperative. Some teens use libraries as safe havens from outside pressures, and "hanging out" has become a major library activity—a noisy and seemingly aimless phenomenon that is full of opportunity for the alert librarian. Contemporary teens tend to come to the library in groups and thus need multiple copies of popular materials so "friends can read, view, and listen simultaneously and have a shared experience."[46] Such solidarity requires creative adaptations of the one-on-one approach.

Then, too, we are now serving a much younger clientele than Edwards envisioned. Her parameters were ninth to twelfth grade, and she spoke of preventing sixth- and seventh-graders from crowding out the teenagers, while *our* clientele grows younger and younger as puberty occurs sooner in every decade and television leads to pseudo-sophistication at an early age. Most YA librarians would now reluctantly admit that although YALSA defines their clientele as people between the ages of twelve and eighteen, they are in actual practice serving the sixth to ninth grades and losing the older readers.

Edwards and Adolescent Literature

When we consider Margaret Edwards and her work in historical perspective, the most striking discovery is the fact that her career essentially predates the beginnings of what we now think of as young adult literature. All of her work with teenagers was done before there were any books of quality specifically written for them. In a sense, Margaret Edwards was playing the game without a ball.

One would think that when adolescent literature did begin to appear, in her retirement years of teaching and writing, she would have welcomed it. But according to anecdotes from those who encountered her at that time, Edwards refused all her life to admit that any but a few YA novels had intrinsic value as literature. True, it would have taken quite a while after the advent of S. E. Hinton's *The Outsiders* in 1967 to see that a whole body of work was developing. Yet in the late seventies she seemed to be still resistant. Deborah Taylor, now Coordinator of School and Student Services at the Enoch Pratt Free Library, remembers speaking with her about YA books at a party during those years. "She was very brusque and very definite. . . . She really had no regard for it. . . . To me, the YA literature was taking risks, and there were good writers, and she didn't want to hear it."[47] In 1987, when asked to recommend the perfect YA books she still did not mention any young adult novel except Maureen Daly's *Seventeenth Summer*, in spite of the twenty years of fine YA writing that had gone before.[48]

Joan Atkinson, Associate Professor at the School of Library and Information Studies of the University of Alabama, shares an anecdote that illuminates in a very human way Edwards's resistance to the new genre. "When she came for our workshop here in 1976, we featured booktalks on three YA novels— *The Outsiders* (Hinton), *Son of Someone Famous* (Kerr), and *Run, Shelley, Run* (Samuels). Edwards had asked me which titles would be booktalked and I told her. When she came, she apologized to me for not having read these books. She said that with her failing eyesight it was difficult to read, and since she was no longer reading for her job, she spent her effort on something other than YA fiction."[49]

It is possible that an additional explanation for Edwards's reluctance to pursue YA novels may have been that she equated contemporary young adult fiction with the type of "junior novel" that had been part of her working years. In 1955 a critic characterized these "sugar puff" stories as superficial, distorted, false representations of adolescence, with stock characters, too-easy solutions to problems, model heroes, saccharine sentiment, inconsistent characterization, and representing the attainment of maturity without development.[50]

No wonder Margaret Edwards saw them as useful only as bait for reluctant or younger readers. Teenage novels, she says in *Fair Garden*, should not be an end in themselves but tools for the development of the reader. And she continues, in an argument that is still occasionally heard today, "In these simple little stories he welcomes the discovery that what he thought were his individual problems are common ones that other teenagers have met and solved."[51] Simple teen romances or baseball stories can be used to teach values and manners to children of the "welfare culture," she believed. Science fiction novels, too, she saw as transitional reading because of their "outrageous plots," and (in a spectacular misunderstanding of the nature of the SF fan) gave them only grudging acceptance because they "lure the nonreader to make a first contact with the library."[52] These "slight" books she saw only as stepping-stones to the real stuff—adult reading.

It is worth speculating that perhaps Edwards's emphasis on the need to guide YA reading came about in response to the fact that there were so few books of value in her time that were inherently interesting to teens and these were buried in the adult collection. She needed to scour the entire library to find those books that she thought might appeal to young people, and then she needed to be thoroughly familiar with the contents so that she could promote them. Young adult librarians today can draw on known authors, formats, series, genres, cover art, and jacket copy to do the selling job that

Edwards had to do from scratch, by the seat of her pants.

An intriguing inversion of the relative value of YA and adult novels is occasionally acknowledged among youth librarians. To some practitioners, adult bestsellers have become the trash from which we want to divert teens, and YA classics the reading goal. "Some adult stuff that's being written now is so self-indulgent, so baby-boomerish, there's nothing there that you would even *want* a teenager to read. Whereas there are people writing about *real issues* in YA literature today," said Deborah Taylor in 1993. "Occasionally, when I have to do a list with mass appeal, I put in one or two of those authors like Danielle Steele because I know that's what sixteen-year-old girls are reading at the bus stop." Yet by 1998 the climate of opinion had shifted, and Taylor chaired a YALSA task force, funded by the Margaret Edwards Trust, that was charged with the annual goal of selecting the ten best adult titles for young adults.

Balancing Reference and Readers' Advisory

In its sunniest passages, *The Fair Garden* projects a world in which teenagers come happily to the library to get a good book. In the dark days of the nineties, Patrick Jones shatters this illusion when he acknowledges the hard truth that many young adults don't want to be in libraries at all, to do hated assignments and endure boredom.[53] Why, then, do they come? As any working public librarian can attest, and as Margaret Edwards and her staff also knew, they come mostly to do their homework assignments. True, they may be attracted by literacy programs, computers, videos, or the prospect of an unassailably virtuous way to get out of the house on weeknights. If there is an approachable YA librarian who has made the library a comfortable place for them, they eventually will also come to socialize and hang out, but the primary motivation is schoolwork, always.

In practice, Margaret Edwards recognized this primary opportunity to initiate contact with young adults on the library floor and to gain their confidence for future book recommendations. However, in her writing she was led by her zeal for reading guidance to infer a competition between reference work and readers' advisory, even describing a future where the information function could be performed by machines.[54]

In spite of the complexities of the reference interview and other aspects of information retrieval, in

Fair Garden she speaks of "answering questions" as the work of technicians, contrasted with what she saw as the more difficult role of a professional book adviser. Thus, she overlooked the primary opportunity to initiate contact with young adults on the library floor, to offer them meaningful and useful service, and to gain their confidence for future book recommendations.

This misperception spread in her rhetoric and through her writings and the librarians she trained. The denigration of "answering questions" extended to forms of information beyond schoolwork. In a review of the 1974 edition of *Fair Garden* Penny Jeffrey says with some bewilderment, "Ms. Edwards never mentions the personal informational needs of teenagers. . . . One gets the impression every problem can be solved by a good novel in which the character has a similar problem."[55]

As the information function came to be regarded more and more the center of library service, Edwards's writings, in an effort to restore the balance, moved further toward a definition of YA work as solely readers' advisory. In her eyes, reference work became the enemy of time and energy and eventually even threatened the very existence of the job. In an interview toward the end of her life, she worried: "I am upset by the library world's increasing absorption with the retrieval of information to the neglect of the promotion of reading. This includes the doing away with YA work as irrelevant."[56]

Although the YA librarians at Pratt inevitably did reference work with teens in the branches, it was given little official recognition for most of Edwards's administration. But in 1963 a survey done by Lowell Martin and financed by the Deiches Library Fund Trustees presented incontrovertible evidence of the proportional importance of the information function in working with teens. Martin questioned 3,578 average or above-average high school students in the Baltimore area and found that over one-half of the individuals using Enoch Pratt libraries were students engaged in school-related reading, that two-thirds of the high school students in the Baltimore area read an average of four books per month in connection with schoolwork and in addition to texts, and that two-thirds of the library service to students was done by the public library, not the school library. Furthermore, although the students reported spending nine to ten hours monthly reading for pleasure, it was primarily newspapers and magazines. They read on average only two to three books a year, and just one of those came from the public library.[57] In the face of this devastating evidence that YA's recreational reading was a miniscule part of their library use, Edwards gave in and in 1961 (two years before the survey's publication, but with the handwriting on the wall— and one year before her retirement) she recognized reference work officially as within the province of YA librarians and began to train them with general instruction at meetings. Later she mentioned the survey briefly in *Fair Garden* but turned its conclusions into a ringing call for more intense efforts to get young adults to read.

Her firm conviction that YA professionals ideally should not have to be bothered with reference may have begun with the shape of her first job with Pratt. As the proprietor of a collection of YA recreational reading housed in the fiction department of the central library, she was seldom approached with schoolwork questions. Cathi Dunn MacRae, who held the same job in the 1980s, confirms that the only kind of school question that ever came her way was a request for a recommendation for a book report.[58] With the backing of the reference staff in Pratt's subject departments, Edwards was able to devote her entire energy to guiding teen pleasure reading and soon came to feel that that was the way YA service should be, always and everywhere.

Nowadays, the balance has indeed shifted as Edwards feared it would, and helping teens with school assignments is often perceived as the raison d'etre of YA services. Contemporary YA librarians realize that school is a teenager's job, and "to do that job well, they often need information and resources not available in the classroom."[59] Reference service can be used as a way to introduce young people to other library services and materials, but it should not be seen as merely a means to other ends. In just the way that Edwards approached her young patrons with book suggestions, librarians now often take the initiative in information service by asking, "Are you finding what you need?" and by setting up user-friendly collections, tutors, peer assistance, homework hotlines and centers, and term paper workshops. "As the teenagers' world becomes more threatening, their very survival, and certainly their ability to succeed, may depend on information," proclaims YALSA portentously.[60]

"Look It Up in the Catalog!"

Information—and the ability to find it for themselves if necessary—is now seen as a vital survival strategy for young people. But Edwards regarded "Look it up in the catalog" as the most hated words in the English language.[61] Faced with evidence that Baltimore teenagers had not mastered library skills in spite of persistent instruction, she concluded that the skills could not be taught, primarily because young people didn't want to learn, and that librarians who insisted on sending them to the catalog were merely lazy—or perhaps sadistic. She believed that the information search should be the job of the librarian, leaving the student's time free for reading, digesting, studying, and writing about the information rather than looking for it. To be fair, it must be noted that a recent *Library Journal* article agreed with Edwards that library instruction is futile. "User education is a marginal, largely redundant service whose aims are better achieved by conventional reference service," wrote Tom Eadie. The trouble with formal library instruction, he pointed out, is that "it provides the answer before the question has arisen."[62]

Nevertheless, in the nineties most librarians working with students are convinced that the methods for finding and evaluating information should always be shared with young people. Patrick Jones declares that the goal is "to provide information literacy tools for every young person growing up in the community."[63] Teaching young adults to track down information on their own, whether it is done in a formal instruction session or on the fly at point of need, appeals to young adults' need for independence and "should be thorough enough to cover not just tools but concepts of search strategy"[64]—a far cry from answering with a disinterested "Look it up in the catalog."

Readers' advisory, not reference, was the center of Margaret Edwards's philosophy of work with young people. In *Fair Garden* she expounds on the goodness of reading with eloquence and conviction and is truly inspiring in her utopian description of the young adult librarian at work, fulfilling the mission of guiding young minds to be better and broader. This objective was perhaps articulated most loftily by her in the staff handbook, "Work with Young People":

In the Pratt Library librarians working with teenagers aim to introduce books to young people which will help them to live with themselves as citizens of a democracy and to be at home in the world. Our goals are a progression from self-realization to responsible American citizenship to belief in the brotherhood of all men.[65]

In other words, the goal was not literary but social and political. "At Pratt it wasn't written anywhere that you took anybody to better and better books," says Mary K. Chelton. "What you took them to was a better understanding of the world."

Demand vs. Guidance

To contemporary librarians, the demands Edwards put on herself and her staff in accomplishing this goal seem impossibly strenuous. She had no patience with desk-sitters, with people who ran their libraries like "Help-Selfy supermarkets." She felt that the librarian should work the floor aggressively, approaching teens in the stacks with suggestions and remembering what every single one had read before. The shining goal was that each reader should be developed to his or her full potential if possible.

Now that the pendulum has swung to the far point of demand-driven book selection, this philosophy can sometimes seem paternalistic in the way it overrides young people's own ideas about what they want to read. Edwards was not hesitant to voice her opinions about teens' narrow interests. "Unless there is a librarian to help him along his way, his haphazard selection of books is not likely to take him far," she wrote. "We fail the boy who finds Erle Stanley Gardner and plans to spend the winter reading all his mysteries if we do not interest him in *All Quiet on the Western Front*, [books about] people of other countries, or such books as Horgan's *Distant Trumpet* and Braithwaite's *To Sir with Love*."[66]

Today's young adult librarian would be likely to argue, "But the boy knows his own needs and enthusiasms; why shouldn't he be left quietly to pursue them and have fond memories of the winter he curled up in front of the fire and read all of ESG?"

It is in this matter of whether we give primacy to young adults' own, often limited, ideas about "good reading" over those of well-meaning and well-read adults that contemporary librarians are most likely to part company with Margaret Edwards—forgetting how she preached that librarians should meet young people where they are. "Our role has changed from readers' adviser to presenter of materials," says Patrick Jones, who believes in centering library service on teen preferences to an extreme degree—no matter how appalling they may be to adult sensibilities.[67] His list of techniques for readers' advising is made up almost entirely of ways to draw out the teen's own desires.[68] He stresses surveys to tabulate YA interests, and the YA collection he recommends is made up of the materials that teens actually read of their own free will: popular magazines, series and genre paperbacks, comics, and only a few surefire hardback YA novels. "Many of us fall back on our own prejudices about what YAs should read as opposed to what they might want to read," he writes[69]—a remark that might have brought Edwards out of her corner with fists flying.

Important as it is to know and respect young adult preferences, at the heart of the mission of the young adult librarian is still Margaret Edwards's vision of the power of wonderful books. Deborah Taylor says of her work at Pratt today, "I've always told the YA librarians here we have to walk a fine line between being descriptive, which is giving kids exactly a mirror of what they already are, and being prescriptive, which gives them a chance to be something better, to try something different in these days when the culture reinforces conformity."

Edwards's Liberal Outlook in Action

In all matters Edwards was staunchly liberal in her viewpoint. She maintained membership in the American Civil Liberties Union, the Americans for Democratic Action, and the League of Women Voters, and she put her convictions into action in her work. "Although segregation remained legally in effect in Baltimore until the Supreme Court ruling in 1954, it never prevented Edwards from establishing ties with the black schools and including the black youth of the city in her program," writes Linda Lapides.[70] Anna Curry, the first black YA librarian at Pratt and later the Director of that library, has described Edwards as her mentor. "I gained a unique perspective of Edwards's ability to put into practice her philosophy of the power of books to bridge cultural differences and empower the disadvantaged."[71]

Societal and economic problems, too, she addressed as a librarian, not as a social worker. Contemporary young adult specialists, besieged with the anguish of teen pregnancy, drug abuse, and homeless and latchkey youths, can take comfort in her advice to temper compassion with a realistic focus on those valuable skills that we *can* offer to help young people in trouble.

In the light of this demonstrated liberality of outlook, the sexism of her language is surprising until we put it into historical perspective. Blissfully unaware of the negative implications of using the universal masculine, in *Fair Garden* she projects an entirely male staff and clientele with her constant use of "he" and "him," when the reality was probably closer to 90 percent female. Such usage, of course, was standard at the time the book was first written (but not at the time of the second edition in 1974).

In other ways as well, the text reflects the sexism of the times, although Edwards herself was a superb example of the feminist ideal. In some places, what seem to be sexist remarks may simply be indicative of the way things were in the repressive fifties—for instance, when she says, "Boys have more interests than girls and do not need to be led carefully from one type of reading to another,"[72] or when she labels booths at her book fair "A Man's World" and "Homemaking" to acknowledge both sexes.[73]

Margaret Edwards was, of course, committed to intellectual freedom for young adults, although with her formidable personality and the strength of her support from the Pratt administration no censor was ever unwise enough to attempt a challenge. In a way this is a pity—Margaret Edwards facing down the Mothers for Morality would have been a memorable spectacle.

There are areas in young adult librarianship today for which Margaret Edwards can offer us no help, simply because they are products of our own times: the ethics of privacy from parents, new ideas about management methods, measurement skills, liaisons with community agencies, the expansion of information technology, and the broadening of the concept of library materials. But when it comes to the land of heart's delight of our profession, the joy in books and young people, and the belief in the transforming power of reading, *The Fair Garden* points the way home.

Notes

1. Braverman, Miriam. *Youth, Society and the Public Library*. Chicago: American Library Association, 1979, ix.

2. Steinfirst, Susan. "Programming for Young Adults." In *Reaching Young People Through Media* by Nancy Pillon. Littleton, Colo.: Libraries Unlimited, 1983, 132.

3. Ibid., 135.

4. Cheatham, Bertha M. "SLJ's 1977 News Roundup." *School Library Journal* (December 1977): 19.

5. Myers, Margaret. "The Job Market for Librarians." *Library Trends* (Spring 1986): 646.

6. McMullen, Haynes. "Library Education: A Mini-History." *American Libraries* (June 1986): 407.

7. Steinfirst, 136.

8. *Directions for Library Services to Young Adults*, Second Ed. Chicago: American Library Association, 1993, 1.

9. National Center for Education Statistics. *Services and Resources for Young Adults in Public Libraries*. 1988.

10. Jones, Patrick. *Connecting Young Adults and Libraries: A How-to-Do-It Manual*. New York: Neal-Schuman, 1992, ix.

11. National Center.

12. Palmer, Carole. "Public Library Circ Leaps, While Inflation Outstrips Spending."" *American Libraries* (July/August 1992): 596.

13. Atkinson, Joan. "Pioneers in Public Library Service to Young Adults." *Top of the News* (Fall 1986): 43.

14. Chelton, Mary K. "Margaret Edwards: An Interview." *Voice of Youth Advocates* (August 1987): 3.

15. Edwards, Margaret. *The Fair Garden and the Swarm of Beasts: The Library and the Young Adult*. Reprint edition. Chicago: American Library Association, 1994, 17.

16. Telephone interview with Sara Siebert, July 6, 1993. All subsequent quotations are drawn from this interview.

17. "Margaret Alexander Edwards Trust: The Lady, the Librarian and Her Legacy." [Brochure] Margaret Alexander Edwards Trust, n.d.

18. Broderick, Dorothy. "Serving Young Adults: Why We Do What We Do." *Voice of Youth Advocates* (October 1989): 203.

19. *Directions*, 12.

20. Telephone interview with Mary K. Chelton, July 14, 1993. All subsequent quotations are drawn from this interview unless otherwise noted.

21. Telephone interview with Linda Lapides, July 7, 1993. All subsequent quotations are drawn from this interview unless otherwise noted.

22. Telephone interview with Sally Estes, July 23, 1992. All subsequent quotations are drawn from this interview unless otherwise noted.

23. Comments by Anna Curry on the first draft of manuscript.

24. *Directions*, 7.

25. *Fair Garden*, 85.

26. Chelton interview with Edwards, 3.

27. Jones, 8.

28. Farmer, Lesley S. J. *Young Adult Services in the Small Library*. Chicago: American Library Association, 1992, 3.

29. Jones, 201.

30. *Fair Garden*, 107.

31. *Directions*, 8.

32. Jones, ix.

33. Ibid., 2.

34. *Fair Garden*, 107.

35. Broderick, 204.

36. *Fair Garden*, 14.

37. Jones, 21.

38. *Directions*, 19.

39. Comments by Linda Lapides on the first draft of manuscript.

40. Comments by Deborah Taylor on the first draft of manuscript.

41. Edwards, Margaret. "Crying in the Wilderness." Letter to the Editor. *American Libraries* (December 1983): 704

42. *Fair Garden*, 13.

43. Ibid., 73.

44. Ibid., 80

45. Chelton, Mary K., and James M. Kosinia. *Bare Bones: Young Adult Services Tips for Public Library Generalists.* Chicago: Public Library Association and Young Adult Library Services Association, American Library Association, 1993, 10.

46. Ibid., 8.

47. Telephone interview with Deborah Taylor, July 22, 1993. All subsequent quotations are drawn from this interview unless otherwise noted.

48. Chelton. Edwards interview, 3.

49. Comments by Joan Atkinson on the first draft of manuscript.

50. Alm, Richard S. "The Glitter and the Gold." *English Journal* (September 1955): 315.

51. *Fair Garden*, 60.

52. Ibid., 59.

53. Jones, 13.

54. *Fair Garden*, 65.

55. Jeffrey, Penny. *Top of the News* (January 1975): 239.

56. Chelton. Edwards interview, 3.

57. Martin, Lowell A. *Students and the Pratt Library: Challenge and Opportunity.* (No. 1 in the Deiches Fund Studies of Public Library Service): Baltimore, Md: Enoch Pratt Free Library, 1963, 110.

58. Telephone interview with Cathi Dunn MacRae, July 22, 1993. All subsequent quotations are drawn from this interview unless otherwise noted.

59. Jones, 75.

60. Farmer, 6.

61. *Fair Garden*, 78.

62. Eadie, Tom. "User Instruction Does Not Work." *Library Journal* (October 15, 1990): 42.

63. Jones, 98.

64. Ibid., 19.

65. Lapides, Linda. "Edwards, Margaret Alexander (1902–1988.)." In *Dictionary of Pioneers and Leaders in Library Services to Youth.* Marilyn L. Miller, ed. Littleton, Colo: Libraries Unlimited, 1994.

66. *Fair Garden*, 85.

67. Jones, 198.

68. Ibid., 81.

69. Ibid., 80.

70. Lapides. *Dictionary*, 15.

71. Comments by Anna Curry on the first draft of manuscript.

72. *Fair Garden*, 21.

73. Ibid., 35.

Bibliography

Edwards, Margaret. *The Fair Garden and the Swarm of Beasts: The Library and the Young Adult.* Reprint edition. Chicago: American Library Association, 1994.

Sayers, Frances Clarke. *Anne Carroll Moore: A Biography.* New York: Atheneum, 1972

About the Author

Patty Campbell has been a critic, editor, author, teacher, and librarian in the field of young adult literature for the past twenty-eight years. She writes a column for *Horn Book Magazine*, "The Sand in the Oyster," which focuses on controversial issues in YA books, and her critical writing has appeared in many literary journals and magazines—such as *School Library Journal, The New York Times Book Review*—and on the YA pages of the online bookstore, Amazon.com.

She is the author of five books, among them *Presenting Robert Cormier*, the first volume in the Twayne Young Adult Author Series, which Campbell shaped as General Editor for many years.

In the past Campbell was the Assistant Coordinator of Young Adult Services for Los Angeles Public Library and taught Adolescent Literature for UCLA

Extension. For ten years she wrote "The YA Perplex," a column of young adult literary criticism, for the *Wilson Library Bulletin*. In 1989 she was the recipient of the American Library Association's Grolier Award, given for distinguished service to young adults and books.